FR. MARK TOUPS

Rejoice!

Advent Meditations
with the Holy Family

ASCENSION

West Chester, Pennsylvania

Nihil obstat: Reverend Samuel Brice Higginbotham
           Censor Librorum
           September 2, 2020

Imprimatur: + Most Reverend Shelton Fabre
           Bishop of Houma-Thibodaux
           September 2, 2020

Ascension
Post Office Box 1990
West Chester, PA 19380
1-800-376-0520
ascensionpress.com

Cover art: Mike Moyers (*Union* © 2020 Mike Moyers, Franklin, TN)
Interior art: Mike Moyers (*Betrothed, Guarded, Breaking Bread, Tabernacle, Holy Family* © 2020 Mike Moyers, Franklin, TN)
Printed in the United States of America
ISBN 978-1-950784-39-4

CONTENTS

How to Use This Journal iv

Foreword viii

The First Week of Advent 1

The Second Week of Advent 33

The Third Week of Advent 63

The Fourth Week of Advent 93

What's Next? 130

HOW TO USE THIS JOURNAL

Daily Meditations

This journal you have in your hands is an Advent prayer journal with daily meditations. Each week of *Rejoice!* has a theme that allows you to dive deeply into the lessons Mary and Joseph have to share about welcoming Jesus into their life. Each week's theme will help you walk closer and closer to the ultimate goal of preparing for the person of Jesus, not just preparing for the day of Christmas.

Since the fourth week of Advent can vary in length, we have provided seven meditations. So, whether the week is two days long or seven, you will have enough content for each day of the season.

Community

Community is a key component in the journey to holiness. Advent provides a wonderful opportunity to take a little more time to focus on your prayer life and grow stronger in friendships on the shared journey to heaven.

The ideal is for a whole parish to take up *Rejoice!* and journey together as a community. You can learn more about how to provide *Rejoice!* to a large parish group at **rejoiceprogram.com,** with information about bulk discounts and parish mission nights with the *Rejoice!* videos.

If you are unable to experience *Rejoice!* as a whole parish, consider a small group setting. Use *Rejoice!* as a family devotion for Advent or get together with a few friends to discuss your prayer and how God is speaking to you in this season.

This doesn't mean you can't use *Rejoice!* as an individual. You can take this journey with Mary and Joseph through Advent even if you are not meeting in a group or talking about it with friends. You are still not alone—Catholics all over the country are on the same journey you are. This journal is a place for you to speak to God and to hear and see all that he has to show you.

Videos

To accompany the journal, *Rejoice!* offers videos with Fr. Mark Toups, Sister Miriam James Heidland, and Fr. Josh Johnson. Through their witness, conversation, and prayer, you will find fresh insights into the details of Mary and Joseph's life and their preparation to welcome Jesus.

The program includes a primary *Rejoice!* video and thematic weekly videos. Each Sunday of Advent, you will get access to a quick video to energize your reflections and encourage you in your prayer each week. Sign up for these weekly videos at **rejoiceprogram.com** to receive them by email.

FOR YOUR PRAYER

Imaginative Prayer

Each day's reflection will end with a prompt titled "For Your Prayer." There, you will be given a Scripture passage to read and a short prayer to pray with. Here is how to pray with these Scripture passages.

Prepare

Open your Bible and read the passage once. Get familiar with the words. Then slowly read the passage a second time. Pay attention to how you feel as you read. Pay attention to which words strike you.

Next, use your imagination to pray with the passage. In his book *Meditation and Contemplation,* Fr. Tim Gallagher, O.M.V., writes, "In this manner of praying, Saint Ignatius tells us, we imaginatively see the persons in the Bible passage, we hear the words they speak, and we observe the actions they accomplish in the event." So, jump into the Scripture passage. Be in the scene with Mary and Joseph. Once the scene comes to its natural conclusion, continue with A.R.R.R.

A.R.R.R.

A.R.R.R. is the next step in imaginative prayer. It stands for **A**cknowledge, **R**elate, **R**eceive, **R**espond.

You have sat with God's Word. You have entered into the scene. Now, once you feel God is saying something to you, *acknowledge* what stirs within you. Pay attention to your thoughts, feelings, and desires. These are important.

After you have acknowledged what's going on inside your heart, *relate* that to God. Don't just think about your thoughts, feelings, and desires. Don't just think about God or how God might react. Relate to God. Tell him how you feel. Tell him what you think. Tell him what you want. Share all your thoughts, feelings, and desires with God. Share everything with him.

Once you have shared everything with God, *receive.* Listen to what he's telling you. It could be a subtle voice you hear. It could be a memory that pops up. Maybe he invites you to reread the Scripture passage. Perhaps he invites you into a still, restful silence. Trust that God is listening to you, and receive what he wants to share with you.

Now, *respond.* Your response could be more conversation with God. It could be a resolution. It could be tears or laughter. Respond to what you're receiving.

Journal

Finally, after picturing the scene with and Mary and Joseph and acknowledging, relating, receiving, and responding, the last step is *journal.* Keep a record this Advent of what your prayer was like. It doesn't have to be lengthy. It could be a single word, a sentence or two about what God told you, or how the day's reflection struck you. Regardless of how you do it, journaling will help you walk with Mary and Joseph this Advent. We have provided space in this journal each day for you.

Plan Your Prayer Time with the Five Ws

Advent can be a busy season. As you dedicate yourself to prayer this Advent, there is no better safeguard than a good plan. Fr. Josh Johnson, one of the presenters in the *Rejoice!* videos, recommends the Five Ws as a method of planning. Here's how it works. Every Sunday, look at your calendar and write out your plan for each of the next six days, answering the following questions: When? Where? What? Who? and Why?

WHEN will I spend time with Jesus?

WHERE will I spend time with Jesus?

WHAT are Jesus and I going to do together?

WHO will hold me accountable to my time with Jesus?

WHY am I prioritizing my time with Jesus?

Having a plan will help you walk with the Holy Family using *Rejoice!* this Advent.

FOREWORD

My mom loves the Blessed Mother. I grew up in a home where Marian devotion was just as much a part of life as fried shrimp on Friday nights and jitterbugging in the living room. I grew up in South Louisiana, which has always been a cradle of the Catholic Faith. There are Catholic churches on every corner. There are thousands of statues, paintings, and stained glass images of the Virgin Mary. However, all the images I saw of Mary were either her by herself, Mary with Jesus, or Mary with Joseph and Jesus as the Holy Family. I never saw Mary's marriage to Joseph depicted. Nonetheless, Mary was *married*. She was a wife. She loved Joseph. Yet I never learned about her marital relationship with Joseph.

My dad reminds me of St. Joseph. As I shared with you in *Rejoice: Advent Meditations with Joseph*, for most of my life I saw Joseph through the lens of a skewed imagination. Every image I saw of Joseph was of him holding a white lily. But men who work hard by the sweat of their brows, as did a carpenter such as St. Joseph, do not typically stand around holding flowers. While there is a truth about Joseph's purity that is conveyed by him holding a lily, this image is incomplete. It shows nothing of his strength and courage as a married man. He was a husband. He *loved* Mary. Yet I never learned about his marital relationship with Mary.

St. John Paul II teaches that marriage is the "primordial sacrament … understood as a sign that transmits effectively in the visible world the invisible mystery hidden in God from time immemorial."[1] What does this mean? Here, the Holy Father is trying to say that marriage is *the* lens for understanding God. If we understand marriage, we understand God. Therefore, to understand the fullness of Mary's identity, we have to understand her marriage to Joseph. Likewise, to understand the fullness of Joseph's identity, we have to understand his marriage to Mary.

I have a passionate love for Mary and an awe-filled love for Joseph. When Mary and Joseph experienced the first Advent, they did so as a married couple. The world today desperately needs a reminder of the reality of marriage. I wrote this series of *Rejoice* meditations because I believe Mary and Joseph asked me to. As a married couple, they asked me.

Of course, each of us is on a unique journey. Married couples may see these meditations through the lens of their own marriages. If so, I pray that these words bless your marriage. Priests and consecrated religious may see them through a slightly different lens, but their celibacy can learn much from a blessed marriage. Whether married or not, everyone is in a relationship with God and others. The questions presented in these meditations will be helpful for your life as a disciple of Christ.

I would like to thank my mother and father for teaching me about Mary and Joseph. Mom, with regards to love of Jesus, you are more like the Virgin Mary than any woman I have ever met. Dad, you embody what I imagine Joseph to be more than any man I've ever known. I love you both, *deeply*.

I pray that your experience of Advent is just that, an experience. I pray that you encounter the persons of Mary and Joseph. I pray that you deeply encounter the reality of their marriage.

Let us begin the journey of Advent by diving deep into Mary and Joseph's marriage.

—Fr. Mark Toups

The First Week of Advent

Holy Love

---◆---

"Lead a life worthy of
the calling to which you
have been called, with all
humility and gentleness,
with patience, bearing with
one another in love."

—**Ephesians 4:1-3**

---◆---

THESE *REJOICE!*

meditations were created to follow the four weeks of the Advent season. We will talk about the first week in a just a moment. In week two, we will intentionally peer into what was in Mary's heart during that first Advent and ask, "How did Joseph love her?" Then, in the third week, we will intentionally peer into what was in Joseph's heart during that first Advent and ask, "How did Mary love him?" Finally, in week four, we will pray with some specific scenes of their marriage.

So let us turn to the first week of Advent. Here, we will lay a foundation for Mary and Joseph's marriage. We tend to look at life through the lens of our own lives. Likewise, we tend to look at marriage through our own experience of marriage. We tend to understand *love* from the perspective of our broken, secular culture. In addition, we tend to look at Mary and Joseph through the lens of our own experience rather than through the Catholic understanding of authentic femininity and authentic masculinity.

Therefore, in this first week of Advent, we will come to appreciate specific aspects of Mary and Joseph's marriage so that we can then appreciate particular aspects of their identity as spouses.

What was Mary and Joseph's marriage really like? How did they love each other? Welcome to the first week of Advent, where we will begin to come to know Mary and Joseph as a married couple.

AVAILABLE

> "O LORD, you have
>
> searched me and
>
> known me!"

—Psalm 139:1

WHAT WE KNOW

about Mary and Joseph as individuals helps us know how they would have loved each other. We know that Mary was completely dedicated to God. According to tradition, she made this vow as a child, a vow which included the exclusive offering of her virginity. We know that her heart was completely *available* to God. The Gospel of Matthew states that Joseph was a "just" man. To understand Joseph as just, we understand that his "whole life [was] lived according to sacred Scripture."[2] As Pope Benedict XVI explains, "A just man, [Scripture] tells us, is one who maintains living contact with the word of God. ... He is like a tree, planted beside the flowing waters. ... The flowing waters, from which he draws nourishment, naturally refer to the living word of God."[3] Joseph's heart was completely *available* to God.

Mary and Joseph loved each other chastely because they were completely available to God. Nothing was off-limits. Because their hearts were completely available to God, their relationship was completely available to God. God knew their urges, longings, and desires, as well as their fears, temptations, and struggles. Because they were completely available to God, their relationship was free from complication, distrust, or secrets.

It has been said that "we are as free as our secrets." Within that wisdom, relationships are as healthy as they are "in the light." When we hide things from one another and do not feel free to share our hearts, our relationships atrophy. When there are topics that are "off-limits," or when we cannot talk about the deepest longings of our hearts, our relationships atrophy. The opposite of being completely available is to hide, protect, or even deny our hearts.

Imagine if you were as free as Mary and Joseph? Imagine if you were as completely *available* to God as they were. This requires courage and trust. Mary and Joseph show us how to live with our hearts completely available to God. Is there anything in your heart that has been hidden or off-limits from him? Is there anything in your marriage, family, or other relationships that has been hidden or off-limits from your spouse or others? Be not afraid. When we are completely available to God, we are completely received by him. When we are completely available to God, acknowledging our deepest desires and honestly admitting our needs, God makes himself completely available to us. Trust the process. Ask him for help. Do you want to be available? Can you ask him for help to be available?

For Your Prayer

Begin by reading Psalm 139:1-16. Read it a few times. Is there anything that you need to bring "to the light" with God or another person? What is God saying to you in the Bible passage? How does it apply to your life? What do you want to say to God?

"Father, I humbly ask you to make this Advent my best ever. Help me to find you deep within. Teach me how to love with the freedom with which Mary and Joseph loved."

What words stood out to you as you prayed?
What did you find stirring in your heart?

DEPTH

"No man has ever seen God;
if we love one another,
God abides in us and his love
is perfected in us."

—1 John 4:12

TO LOVE THE WAY

Mary and Joseph loved requires selflessness and *depth*. To live "in the light" and completely available to God requires maturity and *depth*. Certainly, Mary and Joseph would have enjoyed talking about the simple things of life. Mary would have shared with Joseph her encounters with their neighbors when she drew water at the well. Joseph would have shared with Mary his work and all details of his occupation as a carpenter. They would have discussed the ordinary things of life in Nazareth. Just like married couples today discuss the ordinary things of life, Mary and Joseph would have enjoyed ordinary conversation. But there was more to their interactions … there was *depth*.

There was depth in their individual relationships with God. Because of this, there was depth in their relationship with each other. There was depth in Mary's sharing with Joseph. She would have shared the deeper things, such as all that was in her heart, all that was unexpected in the Annunciation, and how it felt to be carrying the Son of God. Likewise, there was depth in Joseph's sharing with Mary. He would have shared the deeper things, such as all that was in his initial hesitation in accepting the unexpected news of her pregnancy, as well as all that would have been in his heart regarding being foster father to the Son of God. Mary and Joseph would have enjoyed ordinary conversation, such as their day and their work, but certainly there had to be more. There was depth.

Our essential relationships are marriage, family, close friends, and so on. The gauge of how healthy those relationships are is their depth. The reason why most essential relationships struggle is because the people in such relationships have difficulty living deeply. Living with depth can be awkward or uncomfortable at times. Having authentic depth in our relationships is easier when we first have authentic depth in our relationship with God. If not, we may be tempted to grasp in the human relationship for that which can ultimately only be fulfilled by God, or we may not persevere in the vulnerability and trust necessary for depth in our essential human relationships.

The good news is that God is eager to help you this Advent. The first step is acknowledging where you are, what you need, and how you might need help. Whether it is depth personally or depth in essential relationships, the first step is to ask God for help.

For Your Prayer

Begin by slowly reading 1 John, chapter 4. Read it a few times. What is God saying to you in this passage? How does it apply to your life? What do you want to say to God? How is God asking you to go deeper? What do you need from God to help you have more depth in your relationships?

"Father, I humbly ask you to make this Advent my best ever. Help me to find you deep within. Teach me how to love with the depth with which Mary and Joseph loved."

What words stood out to you as you prayed?
What did you find stirring in your heart?

_____

_____

_____

_____

_____

_____

_____

_____

_____

_____

_____

_____

_____

_____

_____

_____

_____

_____

_____

_____

_____

STANDARD

> "Behold, I make all things new."
>
> —Revelation 21:5

OUR ADVENT

journey begins by learning more about how Mary and Joseph loved one another. The purity of their love may seem foreign to what we experience from others or from ourselves. For example, we might struggle to understand how Joseph could have lived the fullness of marriage, while at the same time honoring Mary's virginity. This type of chaste love seems foreign to our experience and perhaps impossible for us to emulate. We are aware of our sinfulness, yes, but perhaps there is more that is causing us to doubt.

Mary and Joseph's love challenges us to consider by what *standard* we ourselves live. In his book *Theology of the Body Explained,* Christopher West writes, "Without reference to God's original plan and its hope of restoration in Christ, people tend to accept discord ... as 'just the way it is.'" Sound familiar? West continues: "When we normalize our fallen state, it is akin to thinking it is normal to drive with flat tires. We intuit that something is amiss, but when everyone drives around in the same state, we lack a point of reference for anything different." In other words, when we live our relationships with "flat tires," Mary and Joseph's marriage, which definitely had "air" in its "tires," seems odd, even impossible. But what if there was more? What if God wanted "air in your tires"?

If we are not striving to love the way Mary and Joseph loved, what are we striving toward? Mary and Joseph loved each other the way they did because of the *standard* to which they held themselves. Their depth and complete availability to God allowed to them to believe that more was possible in their marriage. Therefore, the question for you is, "Do you believe that more is possible for you?"

What is the standard for your personal holiness? What is the standard for your marriage or family or friendships? Goldfish grow according to the size of their bowl. The smaller the bowl, the smaller the fish remains. The larger the bowl, the larger the fish grows. This Advent, God calls you to stretch your heart and go deeper. He is asking you to believe that more is possible. He is asking you to raise your standards of what to expect from yourself. It is OK if you do not know how. Mary and Joseph can teach you. The first step is admitting where you are and giving God permission to raise your standards.

For Your Prayer

Begin by reading Ephesians 4:17-24. Read it a few times. What is God saying to you in this passage? How does it apply to your life? What do you want to say to God? How is God calling you deeper? What do you need to ask him for help in order to raise your standards?

"Father, I humbly ask you to make this Advent my best ever. Help me to find you deep within. Teach me how to love with the depth with which Mary and Joseph loved."

What words stood out to you as you prayed?
What did you find stirring in your heart?

_____

_____

_____

_____

_____

_____

_____

_____

_____

_____

_____

_____

_____

_____

_____

_____

_____

_____

_____

_____

_____

_____

LOVE

> "Love bears all things,
> believes all things,
> hopes all things,
> endures all things."
>
> —1 Corinthians 13:7

MARY AND JOSEPH

loved each other. But what is *love*? Love has become "one of the most frequently used and misused of words, a word to which we attach quite different meanings. ... We immediately find ourselves hampered by a problem of language."[4] To authentically understand the true nature of Mary and Joseph's love for each other, we must correctly define the word *love*.

Saint Thomas Aquinas defines *love* as "to will the good of another." Too often, we try to see God through the same lens we use to see the world; we attempt to understand him through our own limited categories. We cannot do this with Mary and Joseph and expect to fully appreciate the fullness of who they are. Mary loved Joseph, but in doing so, she only wanted what God wanted for him. Joseph loved Mary, but in doing so, he only wanted what God wanted for her. *They only wanted what was best for each other.* They would not have said, "I deserve this."

Let us take this moment to look deep within our hearts as we consider how we love others. We might struggle to love as St. Thomas defines it—and how Mary and Joseph lived it out. How many times do we feel the emotions associated with the word *love*, but quietly desire to get something in return? When this happens, our actions are driven by feelings: we want to *feel* love. We becoming grasping in our relationships. We build up expectations of what we are supposed to be feeling or what another person is supposed to be doing or how he or she is supposed to love us. But pursuing first the emotions associated with love or emotionally grasping at a person so that we can get something in return only leads to us complicating our relationships.

Loving well—the way that Mary and Joseph loved each other—is difficult but life-giving. It is selfless. It requires maturity, humility, and holiness. Then again, what are we striving for? Imagine what our lives would look like if we loved the way Mary and Joseph loved each other. Imagine what your marriage, family, or friendships would look like if you loved the way Mary and Joseph loved each other. This Advent can be different, but it will require us to go deeper. We need to ask God what we really want from him this Advent.

For Your Prayer

Begin by slowly reading 1 Corinthians 13:1-11. Read it a few times. Consider how these words describe how Mary and Joseph would have loved each other. What is God saying to you in this passage? How does it apply to your life? What do you want to say to God? *How* is God asking you to love? *Who* is God asking you to love?

"Father, I humbly ask you to make this Advent my best ever. Help me to find you deep within. Teach me how to love as Mary and Joseph loved."

What words stood out to you as you prayed?
What did you find stirring in your heart?

_____

_____

_____

_____

_____

_____

_____

_____

_____

_____

_____

_____

_____

_____

_____

_____

_____

_____

_____

_____

_____

_____

NEEDS

" O God, you
are my God,
I seek you,
my soul thirsts
for you. **"**

—Psalm 63:1

WE ALL HAVE NEEDS.

Fundamentally, each of us has a need to be loved. We each have a need for friendship, for intimacy, and for being truly known and appreciated by others. We also have desires, or wants. Our desires may or may not be fulfilled; they are not essential to our fulfillment. Since our *needs* are essential to our happiness, however, we will seek to have them met in some way.

In the story of Creation, God said, "It is not good that the man should be alone; I will make him a helper fit for him" (Genesis 2:18). He made us human persons, male and female, to be in relationship with one another. Ultimately, though, no other human being can "complete" us or ultimately fulfill all of our needs. Because we have our origin and our destiny in God, only a relationship with him can fulfill us completely.

As we discovered yesterday, Mary and Joseph authentically loved each other—which meant that each only wanted what God wanted for the other. Their love was pure, and they desired "to will the good of the other." Neither Mary nor Joseph grasped at each other, for they lived centered in God. The purity of their spousal love was illustrated in their freedom knowing they could not *completely* fulfill each other's needs. This freedom allowed Joseph to love Mary as her husband, while reverencing her virginity and her complete consecration to God. This freedom allowed Mary to love Joseph as his wife, while tutoring Joseph as to how to go to God for the ultimate fulfillment of his needs.

Our most painful disappointments tend to come when we expect another person to provide what they cannot. If we expect another person to make us perfectly happy, we are destined to have them let us down. While we naturally desire others to love us, no human being can ultimately fulfill or complete us. Expecting this can lead to deep resentment and unhappiness in marriages and families. It can strain friendships and place an impossible burden on a relationship. It can also lead to grasping at material possessions or status in hopes that those would fill an ache within us.

Mary knew where to go with her needs, and Joseph helped her go there. Joseph knew where to go with his needs, and Mary helped him go there. This Advent can be different, for we will look deeper. Let us begin by asking: What do you need from God this Advent? How can you help others with their needs?

For Your Prayer

Begin by slowly reading Psalm 63. Read it a few times. Consider how you might be expecting someone to completely fulfill your needs. What is God saying to you in this passage? How does it apply to your life? What do you want to say to God?

"Father, I humbly ask you to make this Advent my best ever. Help me to find you deep within. Teach me how to love as Mary and Joseph loved."

What words stood out to you as you prayed?
What did you find stirring in your heart?

_____

_____

_____

_____

_____

_____

_____

_____

_____

_____

_____

_____

_____

_____

_____

_____

_____

_____

_____

_____

_____

_____

HELP

"The Spirit helps us in
our weakness;
for we do not know
how to pray
as we ought."

—Romans 8:26

FOR MANY OF US,

this first week of Advent has been challenging. As we learn more about how Mary and Joseph loved each other, the light that shines in their relationship can illuminate our own relationships. It may feel challenging to consider how Mary and Joseph were completely available or to consider the depth with which they loved each other. We may feel intimidated by the standard to which they held themselves or to love as they did, willing only the good of the other. It may feel sobering to consider that no human being can ultimately "complete" us or fulfill all of our needs.

When we look deeply into their lives, we cannot help but look deeply into our own lives. Here is the good news: God wants to help you. The only way Mary was able to say yes to God and live her life the way she did was with his grace. The only way Joseph was able to love Mary as purely as he did was with God's grace. Mary and Joseph needed God's help. God longed for their holiness. God was eager to help.

The devil usually tempts us with "ninety percent truths." In other words, ninety percent of what we hear in temptation may seem true and good. It is the remaining ten percent that makes the entire temptation 100 percent false and bad. For example, you may be tempted to think, *Mary and Joseph were saints. They were holy. They were called by God to raise Jesus, the Word Incarnate. I am not as holy as them. I cannot be that holy.*

Let's unpack this statement. "Mary and Joseph were saints." One hundred percent true. "They were holy." Again, 100 percent true. "I am not as holy as them." Yet again, 100 percent true. "I cannot be that holy." OK, let's stop right here. What this statement is really implying is, "I cannot be that holy *on my own.*" This is true; you cannot. But the hidden deception that makes it false is that God is asking you to be holy *on your own*. He is not. He is offering you his grace, which alone makes such holiness possible. Mary and Joseph needed God's help. You need God's help.

God does not want to help you less than he helped Mary and Joseph. God is *longing* to help you. Regardless of your past or how often you have failed, and regardless of your present or how much you may be struggling, God is eager to help you.

For Your Prayer

Be not afraid. All you have to do is ask. Today, and throughout this Advent, God is longing to help you.

Begin by slowly reading Romans 8:18-26. Read it a few times. Do you feel any pressure in your spiritual life? How so? What is God saying to you in this passage? How does it apply to your life? What do you want to say to God?

"Father, I humbly ask you to make this Advent my best ever. Help me to find you deep within. Teach me how to ask for help."

What words stood out to you as you prayed?
What did you find stirring in your heart?

_____

_____

_____

_____

_____

_____

_____

_____

_____

_____

_____

_____

_____

_____

_____

_____

_____

_____

_____

_____

_____

_____

_____

DEPENDENCE

"Fear not, little flock,
for it is your Father's
good pleasure to give
you the kingdom."

—Luke 12:32

IF PURITY BEST

describes Mary and Joseph's love for each other, humility is what made it possible. Humility is the interior disposition that reminds us that God is God and we are not. Humility centers us on our *dependence* on God—on receiving everything from him. We receive everything in our lives from him. Humility safeguards us from pride and any false illusions that we can do things on our own, apart from him.

Mary and Joseph's love for each other was imbued with humility, a virtue that is currently in low regard in our secular culture. While we are taught to be "self-made" and "independent," Mary and Joseph lived completely dependent upon God. This is how we can best understand Mary and Joseph's humility—they lived in active, obedient *dependence* upon God.

What exactly is active, obedient dependence upon God? It is not sitting back and passively waiting for money to fall from the sky or food to be magically delivered to our homes. Our dependence on God is *active* in that we play a part. Our part is to share, relentlessly and intentionally, our hearts with God in an authentic relationship with him. God will then reveal our attachments to us and will help us purify ourselves of them. When we relentlessly and intentionally share our hearts with God, we learn to "do whatever he tells [us]" (John 2:5). We are obedient to God, docile to the subtle ways in which he teaches us how to live. If we are relentlessly intentional about sharing our hearts and learning how to be obedient, then depending on God makes sense. Dependence is not an abandonment of responsibility; it is the fruit of purification and a safeguard against pride.

Mary and Joseph loved each other with unparalleled holiness because they were profoundly humble. They lived dependent upon God for everything, including the help they needed to love as they were called to love.

This Advent, God is calling you to an *active, obedient dependence* upon him. This begins when you learn to relentlessly and intentionally share your heart with him. Nothing is off-limits. If you do so, God will reveal what you are attached to in an attempt to stretch your heart and purify your desires. However, to do this you need his help. Again today, we end as we did yesterday. Be not afraid. All you have to do is ask. Today, and throughout this Advent, God is longing to help you.

For Your Prayer

Begin by slowly reading Luke 12:22-32. Read it a few times. Consider the freedom of dependence on God. What is God saying to you in this passage? How does it apply to your life? What do you want to say to God?

"Father, I humbly ask you to make this Advent my best ever. Help me to find you deep within. Teach me how to live in active, obedient dependence upon you."

What words stood out to you as you prayed?
What did you find stirring in your heart?

_____
_____
_____
_____
_____
_____
_____
_____
_____
_____
_____
_____
_____
_____
_____
_____
_____
_____
_____
_____
_____
_____

Joseph's Love

PURITY

"He will come to

Zion as Redeemer."

—Isaiah 59:20

THROUGHOUT THIS

second week of Advent we will intentionally peer into what was in Mary's heart and then ask, "How did Joseph love her?" There is no better word to describe Mary's heart other than *purity*. To understand Mary we must understand purity. Mary's whole person, body and soul, was perfectly pure.

The dictionary defines *purity* as a condition or quality that lacks anything impure. In other words, something is pure if it is free from foreign or inappropriate elements. Mary's heart was pure; she was forever perfectly receptive to God. She was pure, not just because she was purified by God in the Immaculate Conception, but because at no point did anything "foreign to God" enter into her heart or life. She was born pure and remained pure. Because she never deviated from God's will, nothing entered into her heart or her lived experience that was not of God.

As we shall see tomorrow, Mary's purity had profound implications for the way Joseph loved her. Mary's purity has profound implications for us. Mary never engaged with anything impure. Her purity also heightened her sensitivity to God. However, we have not maintained such purity. Sin desensitizes us to that which is pure. As a result, our sensitivity to God's will has dulled over time.

I love epic movies such as *Braveheart* or *Outlaw King*. I love the epic plots, as well as the heroes and their virtue. Unfortunately, such epic movies are often violent. It dawned on me recently that every time I watch those movies, I become more comfortable with violence; I become desensitized to the trauma of war or battle. I no longer see death as death, for I have become desensitized and see it now as merely a part of the movie.

Let me make an application to our spiritual lives. Every time we expose ourselves to things that are "foreign" to God, we become more comfortable with things that are not of God. Over time we become desensitized as we become familiar with sin. We develop an affection for sin and no longer see how dissonant it is with God's will. We rationalize that "a little bit" of sin is OK because "everyone else is doing it." When we sin, we grow desensitized and our spiritual senses become dull. We no longer hear God or feel him as we did before.

Trust the process this week. How have you become comfortable with things that are foreign to God? Have you become familiar with sin? How have you rationalized that "a little bit of sin" is OK because "everyone else is doing it"? Have you become desensitized in your spiritual senses? Ask for help. Ask for purity. Ask God to "re-sensitize" you to sin.

For Your Prayer

Begin by slowly reading Isaiah, chapter 59. Read it a few times. How sensitive are your spiritual senses? What is God saying to you in this passage? How does it apply to your life? What do you want to say to God?

"Father, I humbly ask you to make this Advent my best ever. Help me to find you deep within. Teach me how to live and love with purity."

What words stood out to you as you prayed?
What did you find stirring in your heart?

_____

_____

_____

_____

_____

_____

_____

_____

_____

_____

_____

_____

_____

_____

_____

_____

_____

_____

_____

_____

PROTECT

"Create in me a
clean heart, O God,
and put a new and right
spirit within me."

—Psalm 51:10

AS WE SAW

yesterday, during this second week of Advent, we will intentionally peer into what was in Mary's heart and then ask, "How did Joseph love her?" We have seen that there is no better word to describe Mary's heart other than *purity*. Mary's entire person, body and soul, was totally pure. Joseph loved Mary so he always sought to *protect* her purity.

We have seen that something is pure if it is free from foreign or inappropriate elements. Mary never sought anything that was "foreign" to God. Certainly, Mary was tempted by external factors, but she never gave in to these temptations. Thus, an essential aspect of Joseph's love for her was protecting her from temptation. This meant that Joseph never wanted to tempt Mary in any way, which required that his own heart be free from sin. He had to remain vigilant and sensitized to the movement of God, as well as vigilant and sensitized to the reality of temptation. Due to Mary's essential role in salvation history, we can infer that she was subjected to particularly strong temptations of the devil. When we are tempted, we should imagine how much Mary and Joseph must have suffered in this regard.

I have mentioned how much I love epic movies such as *Braveheart* or *Outlaw King.* Why? Because of the battles. A man's heart has been designed for battle. The problem, though, is that most men are rarely taught what the *real* battle is. Every man—especially a husband or a father—is called to the ultimate battle of protecting his own purity and that of his family. In this battle, his strength is found in God's grace and by the constant choice to say yes to purity.

It might seem impossible for us to love as Joseph loved. We laid the foundation last week. On Sunday, we prayed with the word *available*; on Monday we focused on *depth*, Tuesday on *standard*, Friday on *help*, and Saturday on *dependence*.

We are all called to protect one another from temptation—and not be a source of temptation to others. Spend some time today looking deep within and ask what this means to you.

For Your Prayer

Begin by slowly reading Mark 9:42-48. Read it a few times. What is God saying to you in this passage? How does it apply to your life? What do you want to say to God?

"Father, I humbly ask you to help me to find you deep within. Give me the courage to live and love as Joseph loved Mary."

What words stood out to you as you prayed?
What did you find stirring in your heart?

_____
_____
_____
_____
_____
_____
_____
_____
_____
_____
_____
_____
_____
_____
_____
_____
_____
_____
_____
_____
_____

DIFFERENT

"For my thoughts are not your thoughts, neither are your ways my ways, says the LORD."

—Isaiah 55:8

WHAT WAS IN

Mary's heart during the first Advent? How did Joseph love her? Today we will answer the first question, and tomorrow we will consider the second. There was much in Mary's heart that was *different* from what she expected.

Tradition points us to the writings of the early Desert Fathers, who held that Mary embraced the fullness of perpetual virginity, along the lines presented in Numbers 30:4-6. In other words, the Fathers teach that Mary had intended to remain a virgin and had made such a promise to God before her betrothal to Joseph. Therefore, Mary may have never expected to conceive a child. Imagine her surprise at the Annunciation! Not only would she bear a child, but he would be the very Son of God, the promised Messiah. All of this was *different* from what she expected.

Most of us can relate to things being *different* than what we expect. Perhaps your marriage looks different from what you first dreamed it would look like. Perhaps your family looks different than what you had hoped for. Perhaps your career or job is very different from what you expected. Our lives rarely meet our expectations or look like what we once envisioned.

Mary teaches all of us this Advent where to go with what is in our hearts. We are all called to take everything in our hearts to God. Certainly, we are called to take the particular circumstances of our life, along with our emotions, to God; anything that is different than what we expected. It was Mary's consistency with prayer, even amidst challenging circumstances, that allowed her to experience God with her.

Advent is not always the easiest time of year to pray. It often materializes differently from our expectations. Whether it is dealing with family or loneliness during the holidays, Advent requires us to stay focused in prayer so that we can bring to the Lord whatever may be different from our expectations.

For Your Prayer

Begin by slowly reading Isaiah 55. Read it a few times. Consider Mary praying these very words during that very first Advent. What is God saying to you in this passage? How does it apply to your life? What do you want to say to God?

"Father, I humbly ask you for the grace to find you in the midst of all that may be different than I expected in my life."

What words stood out to you as you prayed?
What did you find stirring in your heart?

Second Week — TUESDAY

SAFE

> " Blessed are the
> peacemakers,
> for they shall be
> called sons of God. "
>
> —Matthew 5:9

YESTERDAY WE

saw that during the first Advent, Mary was dealing with a lot that was different than what she expected. Considering what was in Mary's heart, today we ask: "How did Joseph love her?" Joseph provided a *safe* place for Mary. She felt safe not only physically but also emotionally because she knew that Joseph only wanted "to will the good" for her. She felt *safe* with him because she trusted that Joseph would protect her purity. She felt safe with him because she trusted that Joseph would listen to her heart and, more importantly, that he would listen to the voice of the Lord. Mary, then, could be herself, without fear or the need for self-protection. She could rest in Joseph's presence. With all that was in Mary's heart that first Advent, Joseph was the safest "place" in the world.

By its very nature, the feminine heart longs to be protected, longs to be fought for. A woman longs to reveal her beauty. However, she needs to feel safe. She intuitively knows when she is not safe, when she is not being heard, seen, or received. She senses when she is being objectified and when the motives behind one's look are impure. Joseph was safe. Mary never questioned his motives, his purity, or his receiving her. Joseph's emotional and spiritual maturity led him to be present to the present moment. He was present to Mary, and she therefore felt seen and heard.

Each of us can read today's reflection from our particular place in life. If Joseph could speak to every husband, he would say, "God has called you to be the safest place in the world for your wife. When she is vulnerable, hurting, or struggling, she should feel safer with you than with any other person." This requires strength—a strength that comes from interior maturity rather than muscle, intensity, and financial achievement. To be a real man requires that a man first conquer himself before he seeks to conquer the world. If Joseph could speak to every parent, he would say, "God has called you to provide a safe place for your children. When they question or struggle or fail, God longs for your home to be a safe place for your children to mature through the messiness of life."

All of us, regardless of our vocation, are called to provide a safe place for others, especially during this season. We are called to live in the present moment. We are called to see truly those we are with and to truly listen to them. We are called to love as Joseph did so that others feel safe.

For Your Prayer

Begin by slowly reading Matthew 5:3-12. Read it a few times. What is God saying to you in today's meditation? How is he calling you to provide a safe place for others?

"Father, I humbly ask that you teach me to be the person you have called me to be so that others feel safe in my presence."

What words stood out to you as you prayed?

What did you find stirring in your heart?

_____

_____

_____

_____

_____

_____

_____

_____

_____

_____

_____

_____

_____

_____

_____

_____

_____

_____

_____

_____

_____

_____

HEARD

> " I love the LORD,
> because he has
> heard my voice …
> I will call on him
> as long as I live. "
>
> **—Psalm 116:1-2**

WE CONTINUE

to ask: During that first Advent, what was in Mary's heart? Perhaps there was more there than we think. Because of our great reverence for Our Lady, we might make the mistake of overly spiritualizing her life or circumstances. We need to appreciate her humanity and how she lived her extraordinary holiness in profoundly ordinary circumstances.

Nazareth was a small village of less than five hundred people. It was a simple place. It was poor and humble. There was little exciting about it. Perhaps this is why God chose Nazareth. As with any small town, though, where everyone knows everyone else, it is likely that few things remained private and gossip was commonplace.

The Gospels are silent about what Mary experienced after her miraculous conception of Jesus. Were there whispers among the townspeople, since Mary had not yet begun living with Joseph as his wife? What did the other women say about Mary as they drew water from Nazareth's well? Did Mary ever overhear harsh words or judgments about her? We do not know. It would seem likely that she at least sensed disapproval and judgment, so perhaps Mary's Advent included a battle with what she *heard*.

Perhaps you struggle with whispers of judgment, either from within or without. Many of us hear such whispers when we compare ourselves or our circumstances to others. We may hear within us whispers about who we are or are not, or about what we have or do not have. We may hear within us whispers about how we look or do not look, or about our shortcomings and sins. We might even hear whispers judging us (wrongly) for sins we did not commit or for failures that are not ours.

When we hear negativity, whether from a voice within us or from others, it is easy to get stuck on what we have *heard*. Here Mary can teach us. Her heart remained always sensitized to the voice of Truth. She was able to hear the voice of God amidst any other voices that attempted to disrupt that first Advent. When we struggle with the voice of discouragement, let us turn to God, as Mary did, asking that his voice of truth speak to our hearts.

For Your Prayer

Begin by slowly reading Psalm 116. Read it a few times. Consider Mary praying these very words when she heard the whispers of temptation. What is God saying to you in this passage? What do you want to say to God?

"Father, I humbly ask to hear your voice when I hear the whispers of temptation, doubt, or fear."

What words stood out to you as you prayed?
What did you find stirring in your heart?

LISTEN

"If you abide in me,
and my words abide
in you, ask whatever
you will, and it
shall be done for you."

—John 15:7

WE CONTINUE

to ask: Considering what was in Mary's heart, how did Joseph love Mary? Yesterday, we pondered all that Mary may have heard. Today, we will consider how Joseph loved Mary by helping her *listen* to the Father. Regardless of what she had heard from the whispers of Nazareth, Joseph helped her *listen* to God's words.

Last week, we learned that Joseph was a just man. As Pope Benedict XVI writes, "Psalm 1 presents the classic image of the 'just' man. We might well think of it as a portrait of the spiritual figure of St. Joseph. A just man, it tells us, is one who maintains living contact with the word of God. ... He is like a tree, planted beside the flowing waters. ... The flowing waters, from which he draws nourishment, naturally refer to the living word of God."[5] Joseph constantly "drank" from God's Word. He knew that in order for him to be a good husband, he first had to be a good man.

Joseph's authentic masculinity was illustrated in authentic strength and consistency. Mary was able to trust this consistency. Regardless of what she may have heard whispered about her, she was able to trust that Joseph was listening to God. She therefore felt safe with Joseph.

Life can feel heavy when we struggle with the whispers of comparison, self-accusation, or temptation. We may not be able to name what we are feeling inside, but when we hear the whispers within, we may feel weak or vulnerable. This is precisely why Joseph's being "safe" for Mary was such a gift. Because Mary felt safe with Joseph, she knew that she would always hear the truth from him.

Each of us needs someone to help us *listen* to truth whenever we face temptation, desolation, or discouragement. This is why God said: "It is not good that the man should be alone; I will make him a helper fit for him" (Genesis 2:18). God gave Adam a "helper." Ideally, our spouse should "help" us listen to truth in times of temptation. This requires that spouses take their spiritual lives seriously. If a husband or wife is not first grounded in Truth, he or she lacks the capacity to be consistent, which is essential for the emotional safety of one's spouse and family.

Even those of us who are not married need someone to help us listen to truth whenever we hear the voice of desolation. None of us can walk the journey alone. Who do you turn to? Who helps you listen? Are you consistent enough that others can turn to you? Are you providing a safe place for others?

For Your Prayer

Begin by slowly reading John 15:1-16. Read it a few times. What would your life look like if you lived John 15? How would that impact others?

"Father, I humbly ask you to help me listen to you when I hear the voices of temptation, desolation, or discouragement."

What words stood out to you as you prayed?
What did you find stirring in your heart?

_____

_____

_____

_____

_____

_____

_____

_____

_____

_____

_____

_____

_____

_____

_____

_____

_____

_____

_____

_____

_____

_____

DESIRE

"My soul clings to
you; your right hand
upholds me."

—Psalm 63:8

WE CONCLUDE

this second week of Advent by asking a final time: How did Joseph love Mary? Today we will come to appreciate how Joseph loved Mary by allowing all of his *desires* to be ordered by God.

As the *Catechism of the Catholic Church* tells us, "The desire for God is written in the human heart, because man is created by God and for God; and God never ceases to draw man to himself. Only in God will he find the truth and happiness he never stops searching for."[6] When God created us, he planted *desire* in us. God not only planted *desire* in us, but he created us with desires— namely, desires for happiness, relationship, and communion. Every person is naturally designed by God with the desire for communion—specifically for spousal communion. These desires are good, for they are from God.

Our desires need to be ordered; they need to be aligned toward God. When our desires are ordered toward God, we are able to experience self-mastery. Our desires will not rule us. When our desires are disordered, we can become victims to them through compulsive behaviors, addictions, and an overall lack of self-control.

Joseph's heart was full of the natural desires for happiness, relationship, and spousal communion. However, Joseph was a man of self-possession, so he was not a victim to his desires. Instead, he related every desire to God. In this way, Joseph loved Mary, not by indulging in his desires but by ordering those desires to God. Joseph loved Mary chastely not because he lacked the natural desire for nuptial communion with Mary, but because his desires were tempered and ordered. Joseph desired God above all else. He had possession of himself so that he could best love Mary.

At the heart of most marital tension is some unmet desire, either because that desire is disordered or because our spouse is unable to fulfill that desire due to their brokenness or struggles. The key to a healthy marriage is not a lack of desire but the proper ordering of one's desires. Likewise, even for those who are not married, the key to happiness in life is not the lack of desire but its proper ordering.

Today, we find ourselves halfway through Advent. Once again let us consider: What do you desire? Are all of your desires ordered toward God?

For Your Prayer

Begin by slowly reading Psalm 63. Read it a few times. Consider Joseph praying these very words when he felt any other desire. What is God saying to you in this passage? What do you want to say to God?

"Father, I humbly ask you to help me to find you deep within. Teach me to bring all my desires to you."

What words stood out to you as you prayed?
What did you find stirring in your heart?

_____

_____

_____

_____

_____

_____

_____

_____

_____

_____

_____

_____

_____

_____

_____

_____

_____

_____

_____

_____

_____

_____

_____

_____

The Third Week of Advent

Mary's Love

REROUTED

"But God led the people

round by the way

of the wilderness."

—Exodus 13:18

THROUGHOUT THIS

third week of Advent we will intentionally peer into what was in Joseph's heart and then ask, "How did Mary love him?" Today, let us consider a story from the Old Testament, one that Joseph would have prayed with himself.

The book of Exodus tells the story of Israel's journey from slavery in Egypt into freedom. After Pharaoh eventually frees the Israelites, there is an interesting aspect of the story in Exodus 13:17-18: "When Pharaoh let the people go, God did not lead them by way of the land of the Philistines, although that was near; for God said, 'Lest the people repent when they see war, and return to Egypt.' But God led the people round by the way of the wilderness toward the Red Sea." God intervened and *rerouted* them. While this did not make sense to the Israelites, God knew what he was doing.

Advent teaches us much about Joseph, and therefore much about life itself. Joseph initially thought his marriage to Mary was going to be a certain way. His life was following a particular path. However, when Mary conceived Jesus in her womb through the Holy Spirit, Joseph had to deal with the reality of being *rerouted.* God rerouted Joseph's life and placed him on a new path.

What was in Joseph's heart when God rerouted his life? The first chapter of Matthew's Gospel indicates that there was a lot. Perhaps there were questions such as "why?" or "how?" Perhaps there were emotions of fear or doubt. Perhaps Joseph was tempted to try to control the situation or his life in general. When his life got rerouted, there were all the similar things in his heart that we experience when our lives end up going in a different direction than we expect.

Life seldom unfolds how we think or dream it will. Just as with Moses and Joseph, God sometimes reroutes us from the path we are on and places us on a new, unexpected path. Marriages sometimes get rerouted and go down a path never imagined. Families sometimes get rerouted, struggling in ways never expected. Our careers, relationships, health, and faith in God can all get rerouted.

What Joseph teaches us is that when our lives get rerouted, it is important for us to keep our eyes on God. He often sees things that we do not see. When God rerouted the Israelites, he knew the inevitable victory that they would experience—even though all they could see was the Red Sea and the wilderness. When God rerouted Joseph, he knew exactly what Joseph needed so that he could embrace the circumstances.

For Your Prayer

Today, read Exodus chapters 13 and 14. Read slowly, especially Exodus 14:14. What is God saying to you in this passage? How does it apply to your life? What do you want to say to God?

"Father, I long to trust you with every aspect of my life. Help me to find you deep within. Teach me how to keep my eyes on you when my plans get rerouted."

What words stood out to you as you prayed?
What did you find stirring in your heart?

_____

_____

_____

_____

_____

_____

_____

_____

_____

_____

_____

_____

_____

_____

_____

_____

_____

_____

_____

_____

_____

_____

WHERE

"Return to the LORD,
your God, for he is
gracious and merciful."

—Joel 2:13, NAB

AS WE SAW

yesterday, this week we will intentionally peer into what was in Joseph's heart and then ask, "How did Mary love him?" Again, we ask ourselves, "What was in Joseph's heart?" Joseph's life was rerouted by the Annunciation and Mary's conception of Jesus. When his life was rerouted, Joseph did not know *where* this new path would take him; however, because of the man that he was, Joseph did know *where* to take his heart. In fact, throughout the entire Advent story, Joseph teaches us where to go when life throws us a curve ball. When Joseph dealt with the surprise of Mary's conception, he knew where to go with his emotions. When Joseph dealt with the unexpected news of the census, which required him to go to the town of his ancestors, Bethlehem, he knew where to go with his questions. When Joseph felt the rejection in Bethlehem and was left with nowhere for Mary to give birth, Joseph knew where to go with his fear.

When we are rerouted in life, it is important for us to know where to go with our hearts. We have to turn to God. If not, we may be tempted to try to medicate or numb our emotions. We may be tempted to isolate ourselves and try to fix things on our own. We may be tempted to expect that another human being will be able to provide us with the security and stability we long for. Placing this type of expectation upon any individual is unfair because we are asking another to provide what only God can. When we turn to God, especially when our lives have been rerouted, we are reconnected with the One who has rerouted us. We are able to hear his voice, and perhaps even understand why our life has been rerouted.

Being preoccupied with understanding life's rerouting makes it difficult for our hearts to know where to go. When we become too preoccupied with where we are now or compare where we are with where we thought we would be, we have then placed our emphasis on the wrong "where"—and we can lose sight of *who* is with us. Some say life is a journey rather than a destination. Actually, life is more like a pilgrimage, for a pilgrimage implies God is not only the destination but the One accompanying us on our journey. No matter where you are at this stage of life, and no matter where you are at this stage of Advent, the question for you today is: Where are you going with your heart?

For Your Prayer

Begin by slowly reading Joel 2:12-17. Read it a few times. Consider the freedom of dependence on God. What is God saying to you in this passage? How does it apply to your life? What do you want to say to God?

"Father, I long to trust you with every aspect of my life. Help me to find you deep within. Teach me to trust you with wherever you want me to go."

What words stood out to you as you prayed?
What did you find stirring in your heart?

_____
_____
_____
_____
_____
_____
_____
_____
_____
_____
_____
_____
_____
_____
_____
_____
_____
_____
_____
_____
_____

SPACE

"For everything
there is a season,
and a time
for every matter
under heaven."

—Ecclesiastes 3:1

THIS WEEK WE

are learning what was in Joseph's heart. With many questions, emotions, and desires in Joseph's heart because of the rerouting of his life, today let us consider, "How did Mary love him?" Essentially, Mary gave him *space*. Mary loved Joseph by giving him the *space* that he needed to find God with him in the mist of the rerouting.

We see this most clearly illustrated in the Gospel of Matthew. We read, "Joseph her husband, since he was a righteous man, yet unwilling to expose her to shame, decided to divorce her quietly. Such was his intention when, behold, the angel of the Lord appeared to him in a dream" (Matthew 1:19–20). We may be tempted to read those two verses assuming that Joseph's visit from the angel happened immediately after his intent to divorce Mary. However, there is nothing in Scripture that indicates that was the case. Perhaps there were a few days, or even weeks, when Joseph was struggling with the situation. If that is the case, what was Mary doing as Joseph was deliberating the proper course of action? She gave him *space*. She trusted that he would know where to go with his heart. She trusted that the One who was rerouting him would show him the way. She trusted that Joseph's heart would ultimately surrender to God's will.

What did giving him the space do for Joseph? Mary's trust in Joseph surely elicited deep within him a further desire to do whatever it was that God asked of him. Mary allowed the process to unfold because she knew God was leading it. She gave Joseph space, and this allowed God to move in Joseph's life.

This was all dependent upon Joseph's spiritual maturity. He was a praying man. He was self-possessed and keenly aware of what was going on in his heart. Some of you may long to be able to trust your spouse as Mary did or be as trustworthy as Joseph.

Regardless of our vocation, God is speaking to us today. Mary had to wait *with* God, not just *for* him. During this waiting, Joseph had to find God in the silence. These aspects of the Advent story reveal to us where God is calling us for our own spiritual growth. Give yourself some space today to be alone with the Lord. Trust that in this sacred space, he will speak.

For Your Prayer

Begin by slowly reading Ecclesiastes 3:1-15. Read it a few times. What is God saying to you in this passage? How does it apply to your life? What do you want to say to God?

"Father, I long to trust you with every aspect of my life. Help me to find you in the silence. Guide me as I navigate the seasons of my life and help me to rely completely you."

What words stood out to you as you prayed?
What did you find stirring in your heart?

_____
_____
_____
_____
_____
_____
_____
_____
_____
_____
_____
_____
_____
_____
_____
_____
_____
_____
_____
_____
_____
_____
_____

ADJUST

"We know that
in everything God
works for good, with
those who love him.

—Romans 8:28"

WHAT WAS IN

Joseph's heart during that first Advent? Certainly, there would have been many emotions in realizing the awesome responsibility of raising the Son of God. Joseph's role as a father would have elicited emotions. However, it is not his fatherhood that we consider today; rather, we look at his experience of being a husband. From the very beginning, the Church has taught that Mary remained a virgin throughout her entire life—and that Joseph's marriage to Mary was a real marriage and one lived in perfect chastity.

We do not know what Joseph dreamed of when, as a young man, he considered his future bride. What hopes did he have regarding his marriage? As a healthy, ordered man, Joseph would have had a natural desire for spousal union. After all, the desire for communion, especially within marriage is natural and healthy because it has been given to us from God. In choosing to marry Mary, Joseph may have had to *adjust* any expectations of what their marriage would look like. Joseph was called to protect Mary's purity.

The circumstances of life often require that we adjust our expectations. We may be called to surrender what we experience, or what we will never experience. We may be called to face particular sufferings or challenges. When we have to adjust, emotions can be triggered within us. If we are aware of these emotions, we can turn to God and hand them over to him. Then, our need to adjust can lead to a deepening of our spiritual maturity. However, if we are unaware of our emotions, we will be unable to do anything with them. It is then that we are influenced in ways that we do not see. We may struggle unnecessarily.

Take a few moments to reflect on how you have had to adjust in your life. Consider your interior response to having to make these adjustments. Far too many of us carry disappointments, resentments, and grief from being forced to adjust. Ask Joseph to teach you as you ask the Holy Spirit to reveal how life has made you change your expectations.

For Your Prayer

Begin by slowly reading Romans 8:28-39. Read it a few times. Consider how and when and why you have to adjust. What is God saying to you in this passage? How does it apply to your life? What do you want to say to God?

"Father, I long to trust you with every aspect of my life. Help me to find you when I am called to adjust. Teach me how to live in active, obedient dependence upon you."

What words stood out to you as you prayed?
What did you find stirring in your heart?

TAUGHT

"Love one another
earnestly from
the heart."

—1 Peter 1:22

WHAT WAS IN

Joseph's heart, and how did Mary love him? In Joseph's heart were all the emotions, questions, and needs regarding having to adjust. Imagine for a moment what it was like for Joseph. Of course, Joseph was a deeply virtuous man. He was chosen to raise Jesus and model to him authentic masculinity. On the other hand, men and women are ordered toward marriage, and therein nuptial communion with their spouse. The desire for a one-flesh union within the context of marriage is from God. There is not only nothing wrong with this desire, but if one has a healthy affective maturity, this desire is good.

There was no blueprint for the unique marriage that Joseph had with Mary. Specifically, there was no blueprint for this particular kind of chastity within marriage. In those moments when Joseph needed help, who would have taught him? Mary. She tutored Joseph by the way she lived marriage and virginity. She *taught* Joseph how to go to the Father when he needed help. She *taught* him to let God into every desire and longing. Holiness is *taught*, not caught, and Mary tutored Joseph in his call to chastity.

In nearly twenty years of priesthood, I have prepared hundreds of couples for marriage—and I have counseled many couples who experience difficulties in their marriage. I have found that husbands often do not know how to be good husbands. I have also found that wives often do not know how to be good wives. Neither spouse has been taught. Without a clear Christian vision of marriage, most married couples settle for the images presented by our wounded secular culture. If you are married, I humbly ask you to consider the following questions: Who taught you how to love and serve as a spouse? Who has influenced you in your role?

These questions actually apply to each of us, outside of the context of marriage. All of us, regardless of our vocation, need to ask: Who taught us about how to be holy? Who are our role models? How often are we with them?

Living a life of committed holiness is not easy. Loving your spouse with a pure heart and pure intentions is not easy. Who is teaching you how? When was the last time you let yourself be taught?

For Your Prayer

Begin by slowly reading 1 Peter, chapter 1. Read it a few times. Do you believe the holiness described is possible for you? What is God saying to you in this passage? How does it apply to your life? What do you want to say to God?

"Father, I long to be taught about holiness. Help me to find you when I am called to adjust. Teach me how to live in active, obedient dependence upon you."

What words stood out to you as you prayed?
What did you find stirring in your heart?

_____

_____

_____

_____

_____

_____

_____

_____

_____

_____

_____

_____

_____

_____

_____

_____

_____

_____

_____

_____

_____

STEWARD

> "I will call to mind
> the deeds of the
> LORD; yes, I will
> remember your
> wonders of old."

—Psalm 77:11

WE SHOULD NEVER

confuse *stewardship* with ownership. For example, as a priest, I have heard some parishioners say, "The people own the parish." While I understand what they mean, and I deeply respect their passion in this regard, it is *God* who owns the parish. We are merely its *stewards*, entrusted with the God-given gift of a community of faith. So we must never confuse stewardship with ownership. Since a *steward* is not an owner, he or she lives in an attitude of seeking the owner's guidance on how he or she should care for the gift.

Joseph never confused stewardship with ownership. Joseph was given a gift in Mary by God. Mary was never "his"; she forever belonged to God. Joseph was entrusted with the mission of loving Mary as her husband. Just as a good steward always seeks the owner's direction on how to care for their gift, Joseph loved Mary by seeking God's will in caring for her. He never took from Mary, nor did he act in such a way that implied he deserved something from her. Joseph embodies what it means to be a good steward in being the loving husband of Mary.

We, too, have been entrusted as stewards of God's gifts. For those who are married, you do not own your spouse. You have been entrusted with a mission of loving them, serving them, and helping them along the journey to heaven. Similarly, parents do not own their children; they are gifts from God and ultimately belong to him. God simply entrusts the lives of children to their parents.

We do not own our bodies; we have been given them by God. We do not own our faith, our parish, or our service. We have been entrusted with these things, and as stewards we care for them as God asks us to. We do not own our talents or possessions. We do not own our past, present, or future. *Everything* is a gift. Everything we are and have is a gift from God. Everything we have been given has been entrusted to us by God for our salvation and his glory.

Advent is a sacred time when we prepare ourselves for a person, not a day. We are preparing to receive a gift. The one thing you can do to be ready to receive the gift of Christmas is to learn to receive. Start by asking yourself what you have already received. What have you been entrusted with?

For Your Prayer

Begin by slowly reading Luke 12:48. Read it a few times. Slow down today and ask yourself with what or with whom have you been entrusted.

"Father, I long to be taught about who I am and who you are. Teach me how to be a good steward. Teach me how to live in active, obedient dependence upon you."

What words stood out to you as you prayed?
What did you find stirring in your heart?

_____

_____

_____

_____

_____

_____

_____

_____

_____

_____

_____

_____

_____

_____

_____

_____

_____

_____

_____

_____

_____

_____

Third Week — FRIDAY

RECEIVE

"Therefore, I tell you, whatever you ask in prayer, believe that you will receive it, and you will."

—Mark 11:24

JUST AS MARY

taught Joseph how to be married and chaste, Mary also taught Joseph how to be a steward in the way she modeled perfect receptivity. Mary perfectly received God and his will for her. The definition of sin is when we choose not to receive from God and attempt to provide for ourselves. The Church teaches that Mary was conceived without sin and remained sinless throughout her life. Mary so perfectly received from God that she conceived divine life within her womb.

Yesterday we unpacked how Joseph loved Mary with the posture of stewardship. Today we will consider how Mary loved Joseph by teaching him how to receive.

To reiterate what we saw yesterday: Advent is a sacred time when we prepare for a *person*, not a day. Christmas is not merely December 25. At its heart, Christmas it is not just another holiday or time for family; it is about a person, the Son of God. We are preparing to *receive* a gift. Regardless of how many presents you buy, Christmas is about receiving what God gives to us. So important is this gift, the Church has designated this sacred time to help us receive it more openly. This is Advent, and this is why we are on this journey.

The one thing you can do to be ready for the gift of Christmas is learn to *receive*.

For Your Prayer

Today we conclude the third week of Advent. Tomorrow we will shift our focus toward a personal preparation for Christmas. Our homework today is a bit different. Please review the first twenty meditations and reflect on what you wrote. Take your time. As you review, ask yourself: What has God said to you? When and where were you inspired? When and where were you consoled? When and where were you challenged? Have any themes become apparent?

After you review the previous meditations through the questions above, ask yourself this question: What do you *really* want for Christmas? What do you *really* need from Jesus? He wants to give you a gift that he longs for you to receive. How do you think he wants to bless you?

"Father, I ask you to make this Christmas my best ever. Help me to receive everything you want to give me."

What words stood out to you as you prayed?
What did you find stirring in your heart?

_____
_____
_____
_____
_____
_____
_____
_____
_____
_____
_____
_____
_____
_____
_____
_____
_____
_____
_____
_____
_____
_____

The Fourth Week of Advent

Emmanuel

EYES

> "The angel Gabriel was sent from God ... to a virgin betrothed to a man whose name was Joseph."

—Luke 1:26-27

IN ANCIENT

Jewish custom, marriage consisted of two distinct ceremonies, each held at different times. First came the betrothal, when a man and woman became legally married yet the woman remained in her father's home. Then, after a certain period, the wedding ceremony was held, after which the husband and wife began living together in their new, shared home.

Enter into the scene now. Imagine Joseph taking a deep breath before entering the home of St. Joachim, Mary's father. He has dreamt of this day and has rehearsed what he will say. The day has now come when he will finalize the conversation with Joachim and soon become betrothed to Mary.

Joseph enters the home and shakes hands with Joachim. Mary's father, a holy man, is aware of the timeless adage that daughters seek to marry a man like their father. Joachim's hand clutches Joseph's. Each can feel the strength of the other's soul as they feel the strength of the other's hands. In the silence, Joachim looks deeply into Joseph's eyes and thinks, *Yes, this is a man to whom I can entrust my daughter.* Direct and calm, Joseph speaks to Joachim about his desire to marry his daughter, Mary.

As the two men assent to the betrothal, Joachim calls for his wife and daughter. Imagine Joseph taking yet another deep breath. As Mary enters the room, their eyes meet. Joseph's heartbeat races. Mary smiles with joy, for she has always felt safe with Joseph. Joachim embraces the hands of Mary and Joseph and joins them together. Then, both Mary and Joseph kneel, facing each other, with both hands joined. Joachim chants Psalm 37 as he prays for God's blessing over the two of them. At the conclusion of the Psalm, Joseph opens his eyes and gazes into Mary's. While only a few seconds, both Mary and Joseph feel as if this moment would last forever. Each feels absorbed, safe in the other's eyes.

For Your Prayer

Find some time today to be alone. Find a quiet space. Slow down. Settle your heart. Close your eyes and ask the Holy Spirit to inspire your imagination and guide you as you pray. Imagine the scene above. Be in the scene. Be in Mary's birth home in Nazareth on the day she was betrothed to Joseph.

What words stood out to you as you prayed?
What did you find stirring in your heart?

_____

_____

_____

_____

_____

_____

_____

_____

_____

_____

_____

_____

_____

_____

_____

_____

_____

_____

_____

_____

_____

_____

Fourth Week—MEDITATION ONE

SING

"The child to be born
will be called holy,
the Son of God."

—Luke 1:35

AS WE ENTER

into today's scene, we consider that, through the Annunciation, Mary has conceived by the Holy Spirit. She is carrying the Savior of the world in her womb. She is filled with joy, and she sings the words of her great Magnificat. She remembers tenderly the words of the angel, knowing that on this particular day she will need her own words. Today is the day that she will inform Joseph she has conceived.

She asks for Joseph to meet her in the synagogue. The rabbi is waiting for them. As Joseph enters the synagogue, he is both surprised and intrigued at the presence of the rabbi, who is holding the scroll of the prophet Isaiah. With profound reverence, the rabbi reads Isaiah 7:14: "Therefore the Lord himself will give you a sign. Behold, a virgin shall conceive and bear a son, and shall call his name Immanuel." Joseph's head nods in reverence, for he has heard the words of this prophecy many times since childhood.

Slowly, the pace of Joseph's nod slows until it halts with a piercing stillness. In a moment that feels timeless, Mary's left hands grabs Joseph's right hand. The weight of the prophecy pierces Joseph's heart and his eyes flood with tears. Mary need not say anything as she gently extends her right hand to Joseph's cheek. She gently turns his head toward hers. Carefully and reverently, Mary recounts word for word the details of the Annunciation, the message of the angel, and the reality of the divine Child in her womb.

As if it were instinct, Joseph kneels before Mary so as to kneel before his Savior. Mary is now a living tabernacle. Joseph's only response is to kneel in adoration of the King of the Kings in Mary's womb. Mary begins to sing Psalm 136: "O give thanks to the LORD, for he is good, for his mercy endures forever." Her praise of God is marked with inexpressible joy, and Joseph's awe of the moment is illustrated in his reverence and silence.

For Your Prayer

Find some time today to be alone. Find a quiet space. Slow down. Settle your heart. Close your eyes and ask the Holy Spirit to inspire your imagination and guide you as you pray. Imagine the tiny synagogue in Nazareth. Imagine Joseph kneeling in awe before Mary's womb. Imagine Mary standing with arms outstretched as she sings Psalm 136. Knowing Mary's soul was sinless, imagine how beautiful her voice would have been. Imagine her voice filling every breath of air in the tiny synagogue. Be there, with them, in the moment. Listen to Mary's song. Kneel with Joseph. Be there, with them.

What words stood out to you as you prayed?
What did you find stirring in your heart?

_____

_____

_____

_____

_____

_____

_____

_____

_____

_____

_____

_____

_____

_____

_____

_____

_____

_____

_____

_____

_____

_____

_____

Fourth Week—MEDITATION TWO

AFRAID

> **"She will bear a son, and you shall call his name Jesus, for he will save his people from their sins."**
>
> —Matthew 1:21

TODAY WE CONSIDER

fear. After Joseph leaves the synagogue in Nazareth, the magnitude of the implications of Mary's conception begin to dawn on him and pierce his heart. In the end, we cannot know exactly what he was thinking or feeling. Based on what we read in Matthew's Gospel, he was probably *afraid*: "Joseph, being a just man and unwilling to put [Mary] to shame, resolved to send her away quietly" (Matthew 1:19).

Enter into the scene now. It is late and quiet. There is a disturbance in the air. Imagine Joseph's restlessness as he tries to fall asleep. Alone, in solitude and quiet, Joseph can hear his thoughts, which seem loud and crowd his mind and heart. Whenever he considers the reality of Mary's conceiving, his heart races and he is *afraid*.

During this restless night, Joseph is listening to himself, his own thoughts, his own fears. Exhausted, he eventually falls asleep. Soon a new voice enters his experience. He hears the voice of an angel saying, "Do not fear to take Mary as your wife, for that which is conceived in her is of the Holy Spirit" (Matthew 1:20). When Joseph wakes, he surveys his heart. The feeling of fear has been replaced with a certainty that God is with him. He is no longer afraid.

Joseph kneels by the side of his bed. With his heart certain of the angel's message, he prays and shares his heart with God.

For Your Prayer

Find some time today to be alone. Find a quiet space. Slow down. Settle your heart. Close your eyes and ask the Holy Spirit to inspire your imagination and guide you as you pray. Imagine Joseph kneeling near his bed. You are there. You are with Joseph. You are kneeling there with him. Joseph looks at you and asks you: "Are you afraid? If so, why?"

What words stood out to you as you prayed? What did you find stirring in your heart?

_____

_____

_____

_____

_____

_____

_____

_____

_____

_____

_____

_____

_____

_____

_____

_____

_____

_____

_____

Fourth Week—MEDITATION THREE

GAZE

"He who is mighty
has done
great things
for me, and holy
is his name."

—Luke 1:49

WE CONSIDER TODAY

the conversation between Joseph and Mary following the angel's message to Joseph in Matthew, chapter one. While there is no specific biblical passage that illustrates today's meditation, we can safely presume that Mary and Joseph would have shared their hearts with each other. Therefore, Joseph would have shared with Mary the details of his encounter with the angel.

Enter into the scene now. Joseph walks with Mary through the dusty streets of Nazareth on their way back to the synagogue. During the past few days' of deep intercession for Joseph, Mary had sensed a gnawing fear nipping at his heart. However, today she senses the familiar peace that characterizes her experience of being with him. As they walk to the synagogue, Mary intuitively senses that Joseph has embraced God's call for him and for them.

As they arrive at the synagogue, both Mary and Joseph are flooded with the memory of their last visit here when Mary sang the words of Psalm 136: "O give thanks to the LORD, for he is good, for his mercy endures forever" after she shared with Joseph the news of her conception. Today, as they stand in the exact same spot in the synagogue, Joseph places Mary's hands in his hands and looks deeply and directly into her eyes. His gaze is strong, confident, and overflowing with his trust in God. Mary's eyes rest in Joseph's eyes, for his gaze says all that it is needed to be said. Without words, Joseph's gaze tells Mary: "I am with you. I am not going anywhere."

Joseph looks ever deeper into Mary's eyes, slightly squeezes her hands, and sings to her the first two verses of Psalm 62: "For God alone my soul waits in silence; from him comes my salvation. He only is my rock and my salvation, my fortress; I shall not be greatly moved." Neither Mary or Joseph fully understand the particular details of how the future will unfold. However, both of them have intentionally acknowledged all that is in their hearts—all anxiety, fear, questions, and uncertainty. As they stand in the synagogue and pray Psalm 62, the words of the psalm have become their own words.

For Your Prayer

Find some time today to be alone. Find a quiet space. Slow down. Settle your heart. Close your eyes and ask the Holy Spirit to inspire your imagination and guide you as you pray. Today, enter into the scene, again as if it were the present moment. You are there. You are with Mary and Joseph. You are standing there with them. Mary and Joseph lead you into Psalm 62: "For God alone my soul waits in silence; from him comes my salvation. He only is my rock and my salvation, my fortress; I shall not be greatly moved." What is in your heart as you pray these words?

What words stood out to you as you prayed?
What did you find stirring in your heart?

_____

_____

_____

_____

_____

_____

_____

_____

_____

_____

_____

_____

_____

_____

_____

_____

_____

_____

_____

_____

Fourth Week—MEDITATION FOUR

WEAK

"He gives power
to the faint, and
to him who has no
might he increases
strength."

—Isaiah 40:29

IF MARY AND

Joseph lived in Nazareth, why was Jesus born in Bethlehem? We read in the Scriptures:

> In those days a decree went out from Caesar Augustus that all the world should be enrolled. This was the first enrollment, when Quirinius was governor of Syria. And all went to be enrolled, each to his own city. And Joseph also went up from Galilee, from the city of Nazareth, to Judea, to the city of David, which is called Bethlehem, because he was of the house and lineage of David" (Luke 2:1-4).

Because of the census custom, Jewish families had to travel to their ancestral hometowns. This required Joseph and Mary to embark upon on a ninety-mile pilgrimage to the city of Joseph's ancestors, Bethlehem.

Walking was a normal part of life back then. At eight-and-a-half-months pregnant, though, Mary had less energy. She would have needed more rest than usual. Rest would have been a challenge on the journey to Bethlehem, however. Travel would have taken its toll on Mary's body. There would have been points on the journey where Mary felt her *weakness*.

Joseph was also facing his *weakness*. He would have felt the ordinary fatigue of the pilgrimage. He also would have felt mental as well as physical weakness. Imagine the anxiety of protecting both your wife and unborn child on roads crowded with those returning home for the census. He worried about Mary, the unknown moment of delivery, and how her body would endure the journey. He worried about lodging, money, and providing for his emerging family. The uncertainty of the journey and Joseph's lack of resources would have contributed to his feeling of weakness.

How do you feel about your weakness? Most of us run from weakness, but Mary and Joseph experienced each other *in* their weakness. Their weakness was a part of their journey to Bethlehem.

For Your Prayer

Enter into the scene now. The sun is setting, and Joseph has already spotted a place where he and Mary could make camp for the night. As daylight fades, Joseph builds a small fire. He cannot hide his fatigue or worry, but he does not feel that he needs to. With Mary, Joseph does not have to hide his weakness. In the presence of Joseph, Mary does not have to hide her weakness either. Imagine Joseph sharing his heart. He is completely honest with Mary about his feelings and his weakness. Imagine Mary sharing her heart. She is completely honest with Joseph about her feelings and her weakness. You are there with them. Imagine them looking at you and asking how you feel about your own weakness.

What words stood out to you as you prayed?
What did you find stirring in your heart?

_____

_____

_____

_____

_____

_____

_____

_____

_____

_____

_____

_____

_____

_____

_____

_____

_____

_____

_____

_____

RELY

> "Cast all your
> anxieties on him,
> for he cares
> about you."

—1 Peter 5:7

WITH NAZARETH

far behind them and Bethlehem just off on the horizon, Mary was beginning to indicate that she would deliver any day now. She was quiet, drawn into a deep place of contemplation for all that was unfolding. There was much she did know, but so much more she did not know. She had to *rely* on God.

With each step up the mountainous terrain toward Bethlehem, Joseph, too, had to *rely* on God. There was much he did have, but so much more he did not have. He did not have answers to questions. He did not have much to provide for his wife. He did not have experience as a father to raise the Son of God. He had to rely on the Lord.

Weakness forces us to rely. Weakness may force us to rely on others or may force us to rely on God. One of the reasons many of us do not like our weakness is because we resist the vulnerability of having to rely on someone else. In our weakness, we are out of control. Most of us are afraid of vulnerability because it has not been a safe place for us in the past.

If we are to *rely* on someone, we must trust them. Mary and Joseph knew the heart of the Father. They trusted him. They also trusted each other and thus felt safe in exposing their weakness. Considering the awesome circumstances of carrying and soon caring for the Son of God, Mary and Joseph had one, and only one choice—to rely on God.

For Your Prayer

Enter into the scene now. Imagine Joseph taking one last breath before he and Mary begin ascending the mountain up to Bethlehem. With his gaze lifting upward, tears flood his eyes. As he takes one deliberate step at a time, the pressure on his aching feet force him to rely on God. Joseph begins to admit to himself that he does not know where he is taking them when he arrives in the town. After only a few feet, he stops in silence. He feels inadequate and must rely on God. Mary is riding on the donkey, but the rhythmic sway of the flat roads has been replaced with an upward climb. The exhausted donkey is growing weaker by the hour, and their food supply has become stretched thin. Mary is not worried, as she is aware of her reliance on God. Imagine that you are there with them. Imagine you are walking alongside of Mary. She looks at you and asks, "Where are you being asked to rely on God?"

What words stood out to you as you prayed?
What did you find stirring in your heart?

_____

_____

_____

_____

_____

_____

_____

_____

_____

_____

_____

_____

_____

_____

_____

_____

_____

_____

_____

_____

_____

Fourth Week—MEDITATION SIX

FULFILL

> "And you shall be my people, and I will be your God."

—Jeremiah 30:22

MARY AND JOSEPH

know they can rely on God because he had promised them he would provide. When God makes a promise, he always *fulfills* it. Thousands of years prior to this epic pilgrimage to Bethlehem, God promised the Israelites that they would be his people and he would be their God (see Jeremiah 30:22). He promised that he would never abandon them (see Deuteronomy 31:6)—and that he would *fulfill* his promise to send a Savior.

For thousands of years Israel waited. She waited while she found her identity and waited still more when she lost her sense of whose she was. She waited when she was in her homeland and waited still more when she was enslaved in exile. She waited in Israel. She waited in Egypt. She waited in Babylon. She waited when the Romans occupied her. Israel waited for the day when she would see God's face and hear his voice. Israel waited for a person to fulfill the promise made to the prophet Isaiah:

> The Spirit of the Lord God is upon me, because the Lord has anointed me to bring good tidings to the afflicted; he has sent me to bind up the brokenhearted, to proclaim liberty to the captives, and the opening of the prison to those who are bound; to proclaim the year of the Lord's favor, and the day of vengeance of our God; to comfort all who mourn (Isaiah 61:1).

Today, let us enter into the scene. Imagine that you are there. You are walking with Mary and Joseph as they frantically find a cave that will provide shelter for Jesus' birth. You are there. Joseph escorts Mary into the cave, and then with tenderness and strength gently guides Mary as she lies down. The cave is safe and dry, but it is poor and meager. _____

You are there. You can feel the damp, cool, earthen floor. You can feel the anticipation that fills the air. The time has come to fulfill the promise. There is a person, a real person, inside the womb of Mary who will fulfill every promise ever made. The child to be born is not merely a cute baby. He is the One who is the fulfillment of every promise.

For Your Prayer

Find some time today to be alone. Find a quiet space. Slow down. Settle your heart. Close your eyes and ask the Holy Spirit to guide you as you pray. Visualize the scene. Be *in* the scene. Be *with* Mary and Joseph as if it is now happening in the present moment.

What words stood out to you as you prayed?
What did you find stirring in your heart?

_____

_____

_____

_____

_____

_____

_____

_____

_____

_____

_____

_____

_____

_____

_____

_____

_____

_____

_____

Fourth Week—MEDITATION SEVEN

NEXT

"This will be a sign
for you: you will find
a baby wrapped in
swaddling cloths and
lying in a manger."

—Luke 2:12

AS SOON AS MARY

gave birth to Jesus, her firstborn son, she "wrapped him in swaddling cloths, and laid him in a manger" (Luke 2:7). Over the previous nine months, Mary's body prepared for the birth of the infant in her womb. During those nine months, however, Mary prepared for much more than the day of her son's birth; she prepared for a new life defined by her identity as the mother of the Messiah. Mary was not preparing for a day (Christmas); she was preparing for a person (Jesus). So, the very next thing she did was wrap him in the same cloths one would place on any baby, yet at the same time recognizing that this was more than just any baby—this was the Messiah.

Most of the world spends the first twenty-four days of December getting ready for a day, the twenty-fifth. How soon, though, the world moves on to what is *next*. For most, Christmas is just a holiday. New Year's Day is the *next* holiday that follows soon after. The world quickly moves on. The Christmas trees begin to be removed on the twenty-sixth. The decorations get put away, and the next set of decorations are readied. Because our culture focuses on events rather than people, it is always gearing up for the next big celebration.

Contrast this with Mary and Joseph at the Nativity. They were not preparing for a day; they were preparing for a person. Furthermore, this person would change their lives—and the lives of everyone—forever. Mary's focus is on the person. She wraps Jesus in swaddling cloths because she knows full well that this tiny person is the most important thing in life. The next thing for Mary is Jesus … the Messiah … the Savior. Mary did not move on to the next diversion.

What is *next* for you? What is your interior attitude today? Are you committed to the person of Jesus … or are you feeling the lure to move on to the next day on the calendar? Spend some time with Mary. Hold the very child that she held. The more you experience the grace of the Nativity, the easier it will be to keep your eyes focused on what is next—Jesus.

For Your Prayer

Imagine how Mary and Joseph would have sung psalms during the most silent of nights outside Bethlehem. Begin by slowly reading Psalm 80. Consider the sweetness of their singing. Now, prayerfully imagine the scene in Luke 2:7. Be *in* the scene. Be *with* Mary as she wraps Jesus in swaddling cloths. Now, ask Mary if *you* too can hold her son, and behold the Savior of the World.

What words stood out to you as you prayed? What did you find stirring in your heart?

_____
_____
_____
_____
_____
_____
_____
_____
_____
_____
_____
_____
_____
_____
_____
_____
_____
_____
_____
_____
_____
_____

"For to us a child is born,
to us a son is given."

—Isaiah 9:6

NOTES

1 General Audience, Wednesday, February 20, 1980.

2 Pope Benedict XVI, *Jesus of Nazareth: The Infancy Narratives*, 39.

3 Ibid.

4 *Deus Caritas Est.* 1.

5 *Deus Caritas Est* 1.

6 *Catechism of the Catholic Church* (CCC) 27.

What's Next?

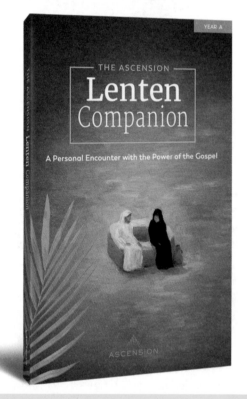

A Trilogy of Advent Meditations with **Mary, Joseph** and the **Holy Family**

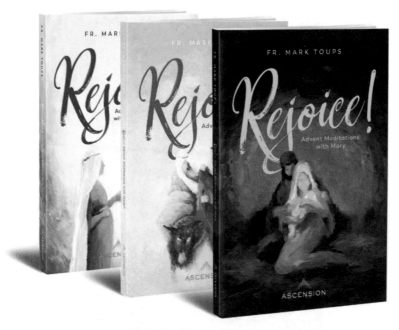

Rejoice! by Fr. Mark Toups

Do you want to experience real transformation this Advent? The **Rejoice!** Advent Meditations Series from Ascension presents a new way to approach Advent. Each journal presents a uniquely personal way to approach this blessed season, with Mary and Joseph as they prepare for the birth of their Son, the Savior of the world.

In these beautiful journals, you will engage in daily reflection, prayer, find a simple path to peace and joy during this busy and often hectic season, and walk closely with the people who prepared to welcome Christ at the very first Christmas.

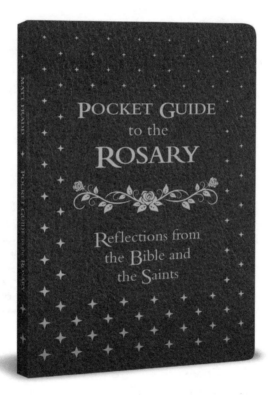